CREATURES ALL AROUND US

What Bit Me?

by D. M. Souza

Carolrhoda Books, Inc./Minneapolis

Many of the photos in this book show the insects larger than life size. The degree of magnification varies.

Library of Congress Cataloging-in-Publication Data

Souza, D. M. (Dorothy M.)
    What bit me? / by D. M. Souza.
        p.   cm.
    Includes index.
    Summary: Describes the physical characteristics, life cycle, and habits of various biting and stinging insects.
    ISBN 0-87614-440-7
    1. Insects—Juvenile literature. 2. Insect pests—Juvenile literature. 3. Bites and stings—Juvenile literature.
[1. Insects. 2. Insect pests. 3. Bites and stings.] I. Title.
QL467.2.S69   1991
595.7′053—dc20   90-38291
                                                        CIP
                                                         AC

Manufactured in the United States of America

1 2 3 4 5 6 7 8 9 10 00 99 98 97 96 95 94 93 92 91

A doodlebug waits in its pit for an ant to fall in.

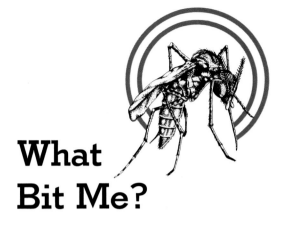

What Bit Me?

Insects lead dangerous lives. If they are not being zapped by humans, they are being hunted, chased, or ambushed by other insects and small animals.

Ants, for example, are often trapped by the doodlebug, which is the young, or **larva**, of an insect called the ant lion. The doodlebug digs a pit at the base of a tree and waits for an ant to stumble in. When one does, the doodlebug tosses small stones at the ant with its head or wiggles its leg until dirt falls on the victim. Then the doodlebug grabs the ant and feasts on it. Ants must always be on the lookout for doodlebugs.

Many insects have weapons to help defend themselves against attackers. Many bees and wasps have stingers on the ends of their bodies. When necessary, the insects can jab their stingers into an attacker. They then release a poison through the tube that can kill or paralyze other insects or spiders—or make us yell "ouch."

Some insects feed on or in the bodies of other living insects, spiders, or larger animals. Insects that do this are called **parasites** (PAR-uh-sytes). The creatures that they feed on are known as **hosts**.

Parasites may lay their eggs on or in their hosts, and some may even spend their entire lives there. The larvae of many flies and wasps are among the insects that act as parasites.

Tiny red mites are living on the body of this grasshopper. They are parasites, dependent on their grasshopper host.

4

Once in a while, parasites such as mites, ticks, fleas, or lice may land on us. With their piercing-sucking mouthparts, they feast on our blood or body tissues. We may not even know they are on us until their bites begin to itch or swell.

What some of these creatures do, and how they do it, may be of interest to you.

A tick is a parasite that often feeds on humans. Some ticks can cause us to become ill.

This female mosquito is feeding on someone's arm.

The Humming, Singing Insect

You are almost asleep when a mosquito begins humming and singing in your ear. No matter how many times you toss and turn, swing your arms, or swat the air around you, the insect keeps coming back. How did it find you, and what does it want?

Scientists believe the mosquito can sense the warmth of your body. This lets it know a blood meal is close by. Females, the only mosquitoes that bite, occasionally need to feed on blood. Just as milk helps your bones grow and become stronger, blood helps young mosquito eggs develop.

When the female mosquito flying around you lands, she uses her drill-like beak, or **proboscis** (pro-BAH-sis), to puncture your skin. This beak is sharp enough to pierce the leathery skin of a frog or the scales of a snake. You probably won't feel the proboscis going into your skin, but you will feel the effects of the mosquito's saliva. This saliva thins your blood and keeps it from clotting as the mosquito pumps it into her own body.

If you do not disturb her, eventually the mosquito will draw out most of her saliva. However, if you swat her before she is finished, the saliva that she leaves will make your bite itch and swell. This is your body's way of reacting to a substance that does not belong in it.

The mosquito's body is filled with blood that she has drawn out of her victim's arm.

In spring, the female mosquito searches for water in which to lay her eggs. A rain puddle, a tin can holding a bit of water, a vase of flowers, a fish pond—any drop of fresh water will do. Most mosquitoes lay from one hundred to four hundred eggs in a boat-shaped clump that floats on the water. These eggs hatch into larvae that are often called **wrigglers**.

Mosquito eggs floating on water. These eggs will soon hatch into larvae called wrigglers.

Wrigglers live below the surface of the water. From time to time, they will come up for air.

Each wriggler is shaped like a miniature submarine, with a tube (called a siphon) near the end of its body. This tube looks like a periscope. From time to time, a wriggler comes to the surface of the water, pokes up its "periscope," and draws in a supply of air. Then it returns below the surface to nibble on plants. For now, the wriggler has chewing mouthparts. These will change to piercing-sucking ones when the wriggler becomes an adult mosquito.

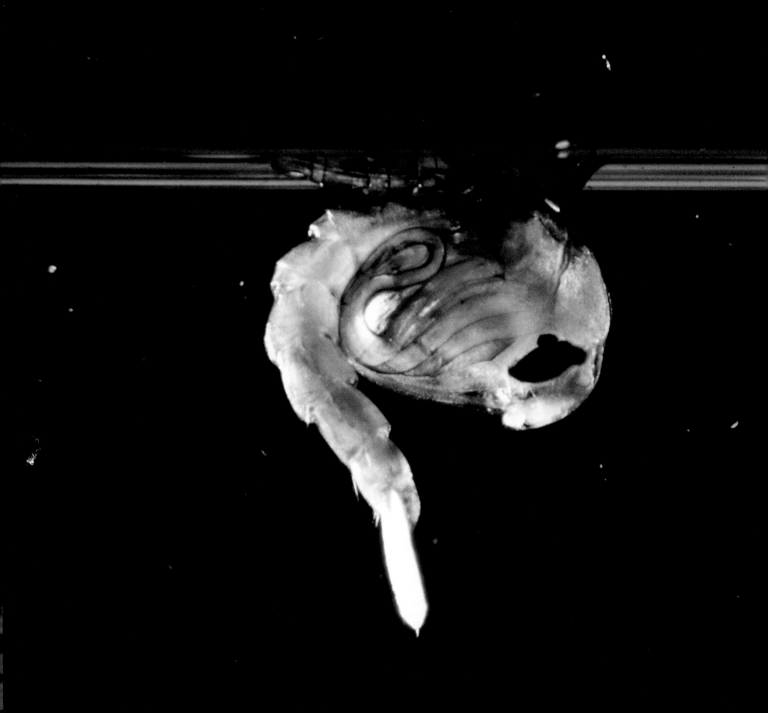

*Mosquito pupae are
often called tumblers,
because they move
by rolling over
and over.*

After about two weeks
(depending on the weather
and the type of mosquito),
the wriggler passes into the
next stage of its develop-
ment—the pupal stage. The
pupa (PYOO-pah) moves
around in the water by
rolling over and over again.
For this reason, the mosquito
pupa is sometimes known
as a **tumbler**.

13

Tumblers have large heads and small tails, do not eat, and look like commas. They breathe air through two horn-like structures called trumpets. After about three days, a tumbler is ready to leave its water nursery. It rests near the surface of the water. Soon its outer skin, or **cuticle** (KYOO-tih-kuhl), cracks open due to the pressure of the full-grown body within. Slowly a wet mosquito crawls out. Before it can fly away, it must wait about 10 minutes for its wings to dry.

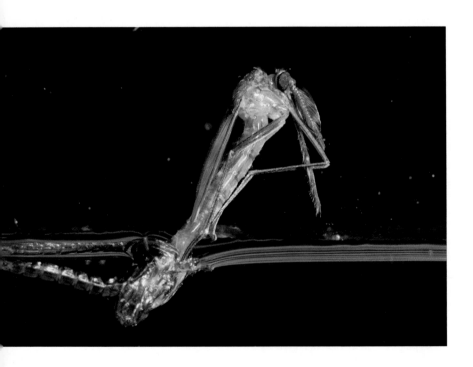

Left: *This tumbler is breaking out of its cuticle. It will emerge as a full-grown mosquito.*

Right: *Male mosquitoes, such as the one pictured here, have feathery antennae.*

The first new mosquitoes to fly are the males. Unlike the females, which have plain antennae, the males have feathery ones. They use their antennae to pick up the sounds of females, which are the only mosquitoes that hum and buzz. Females make noise by vibrating the thin scales in front of their **spiracles** (SPIHR-uh-kuhlz), or breathing holes.

The males, which have poorly developed mouthparts, feed on plant juices. They bother no one and try to avoid being eaten by birds, frogs, and other insects. Within a week of leaving the water, the males die. The females may live as long as a month, feasting on blood and plant juices and laying their eggs.

Mosquitoes belong to the same group of insects as flies. In Spanish, the word *mosca* means "fly," and *mosquito* "little fly." Like flies, mosquitoes live both indoors and out. In warm tropical areas, some mosquitoes are carriers of serious diseases such as yellow fever and malaria. Most of the mosquitoes you meet, however, will simply pester you by humming and singing in your ear and trying to find food on some part of your body.

Although mosquitoes in some countries carry diseases, most of the ones you meet will simply pester you.

Bedbugs got their name because they like to live in warm places.

A Parade of Bugs

Some people call all insects *bugs*, but actually only the group known as **Hemiptera** (heh-MIP-tuh-ruh), or half-wings, should truly be called bugs. This group includes over 55,000 different varieties of insects. While most bugs feed on plant juices, other insects, or other animals, a few may prefer to dine on you.

Bedbugs, for example, like to hitchhike on clothing, furniture, or luggage to get into warm places such as hotel or motel rooms. They spend their days sleeping in rugs or bedding. At night they crawl out in search of food.

17

These insects are difficult to spot. Some are smaller than ¼ inch long. Bedbugs are brownish in color, broad, and flat. They cannot fly but must crawl to dinner.

Once a bedbug reaches a person or animal, it pierces its victim's skin with its long proboscis and begins sipping. Both male and female bedbugs do this, although females usually take in twice as much blood as males. As it sips, the bedbug injects its saliva into the blood of its host. The saliva causes itching and swelling. In a few minutes, the bedbug turns a dull red, lets go of its victim, and falls off. Then it slowly crawls away to digest its meal. Digestion may take several days.

Female bedbugs lay four or five eggs a day. If the temperature is warm enough, they may lay as many as two hundred in a lifetime. The mother usually attaches her eggs to rugs, furniture, or bedding with a sticky substance that hardens after a few minutes.

In about six days, the eggs hatch into **nymphs**. These nymphs look very much like their parents. After **molting**, or shedding their skin, several times, nymphs become adults and begin searching for their own blood meals.

If something bites your toes while you're swimming, it could be a giant water bug like this one.

If you have ever gone swimming in a stream or pond, you may have met insects from the group known as water bugs. These bugs keep their piercing-sucking mouthparts ready, and if they spot a toe or two, they may attack. Because of this habit, they have earned the nickname "toe-biters."

Some giant water bugs grow to be as big as 3 inches long and 1 inch or more wide. They feed on insects, tadpoles, and small fish. Usually giant water bugs hide under leaves near the bottom of a pond or stream. When a fish—or a toe—comes by, they move forward. They grab the victim with their front legs, stab it with their beaks, and wait for their poisonous saliva to act.

In late summer, if their ponds dry up, some water bugs take to the air. They search for piles of fallen leaves where they can spend the winter. If one of them spots a light in a house or garden, it may fly into it. That habit has won this type of water bug the nickname "electric light bug."

You wouldn't enjoy meeting this assassin bug nymph. Assassin bugs use their legs to hold their victims while they draw blood with their piercing-sucking beaks.

Almost every country in the world has assassin bugs. There are about 2,500 different kinds. Many assassin bugs are black or dark brown. They have piercing-sucking beaks and strong legs that they use to grasp their victims. Above the lower part of each leg is a special pad with many—perhaps 80,000—oily, sticky hairs. These help the bugs hold on to their victims while they stab them with their beaks and inject poison.

Years ago, some assassin bugs were welcomed indoors when it was discovered that they attacked bedbugs. Unfortunately for the assassin bugs, they made the mistake of also attacking the owner of the house. After that, like most other bugs, they were added to the list of pests.

Assassin bugs are found in most countries. Wherever they go, they're unwelcome guests.

This flea prefers to feed on dogs, but it will settle for other animals.

Skinny and Wingless

For a long time dogs, cats, bats, birds, and people have been itching and scratching because of fleas. As a matter of fact, these insects have been sipping blood from other creatures for over 40 million years.

There are over one thousand different kinds of fleas, and all have favorite meals. Some prefer to snack on rats, hogs, or skunks, others on dogs or cats, still others on you or me. Most fleas, however, will hop on any animal if their favorite one is not around.

Fleas are flat like ice cream sticks and have no wings. They have two short antennae and six long legs that end in claws. Some are weak-sighted and are only able to see 1 inch away. Bat fleas have no eyes at all.

If you are sitting on the grass near a resting flea, the insect's antennae will quickly sense your body heat. The flea will turn around and, using its hind legs, will jump aboard you. It can high-jump 8 inches and broad-jump 13. This may not seem far, but considering the flea's size, it's amazing. If you could do as well, you would be able to jump 800 feet!

Once it lands, the flea is able to slip through your jacket, sweater, or other clothing because of its narrow body. With its pointed beak, it pierces your skin and injects saliva to thin your blood and keep it from clotting. Then it sips a meal of blood. The amount of flea saliva that makes your bite itch is smaller than a pinpoint. It would take more than 1½ million fleas to produce enough saliva to equal a drop of water.

Although they can't fly away from you, fleas are hard to catch because they are excellent jumpers.

24

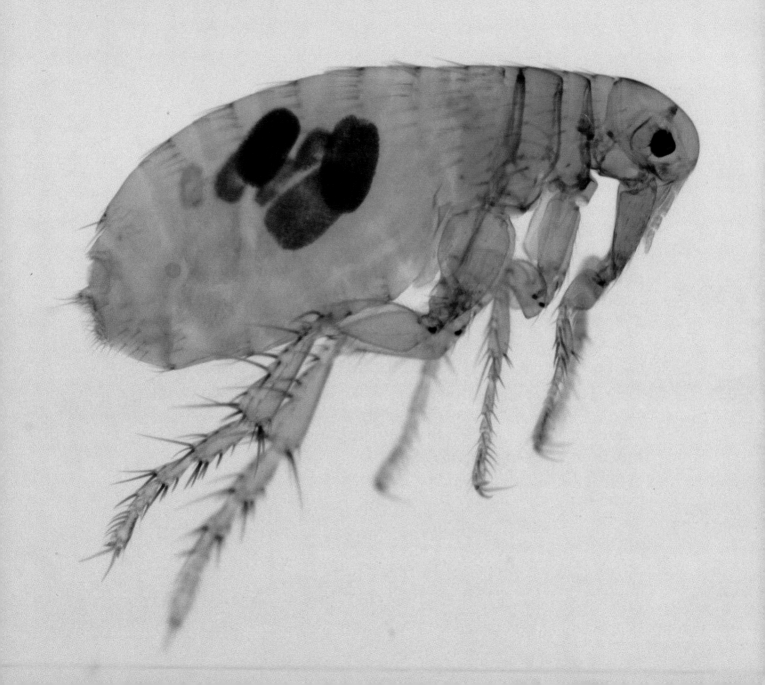

After feasting, the female flea may lay her eggs, sometimes 8 at a time. She is not particular about where she drops them. Some fall to the ground or end up in an animal's den or nest. In a few months one female may release as many as 450 eggs.

Inside its egg case, each flea larva has a sharp point on its back. It moves around inside the case, pressing this point against the wall until the case is cut. Then out comes a white, hairy, legless larva. It has chewing mouthparts and feeds on adult flea droppings or other tidbits found in dusty, dirty places. After about two weeks, it spins a cocoon and turns into a pupa, remaining in this stage for about three more weeks. Finally it becomes an adult. Adult male fleas are smaller and thinner than adult females, but their appetites are just as big.

Fleas spend most of their adult lives on the body of their chosen hosts. Their thinness makes it easy for them to slip quickly out of sight. As they crawl through jungles of fur, small backward-pointing hairs, or **spines**, along their sides help them move forward.

It's possible that your dog or cat might capture a flea by biting and swallowing it. If the flea has a tapeworm living within it, your pet might end up with tapeworms, too. Other fleas, especially those living on rats and wild animals, carry deadly diseases.

As clever and unique as these insects are, it's no wonder their talents do not make them very popular.

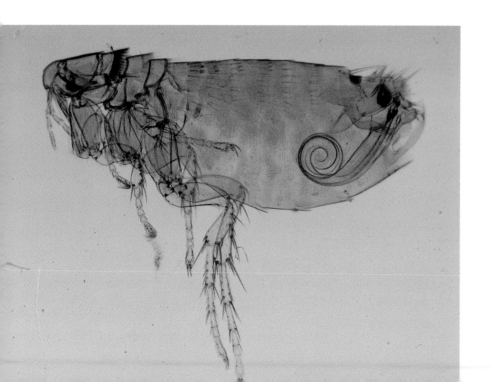

Male fleas such as this one are smaller than females, but their appetites are just as big.

Different types of lice prefer different types of hosts. This louse lives on hogs.

Hangers-On

A louse is another of those insects you would rather not meet. It is wing-less and slightly larger than a flea and has an almost flat body. Like the flea, it has poorly developed eyes and likes to sip blood.

There are about 500 different kinds of lice that feed on the blood of mammals. Some stay only on mice, others only on dogs or cats. One type lives behind the ears of elephants. Three different types like parts of our bodies.

The head louse is gray and spends its entire life on the human scalp. When it first pokes its mouthparts into your head, you may not feel the stab. But in minutes, after the louse's saliva mixes with your blood, your scalp will itch. The head louse does not stuff itself at any one feeding, but snacks every few hours. It drinks only blood and cannot survive for long if it falls to the ground.

You may not feel the bite of a head louse, but it will make you itch.

*Head lice and their
eggs, or nits, are hard
to get out of your hair.*

When females lay their small, white eggs, or **nits**, they attach them to hairs with a cementlike substance. The eggs hatch into nymphs in as few as five days and join the adults in feeding on the scalp. After molting several times, they become adults and, in less than a month, begin laying eggs of their own in the same head of hair. Strong claws on their feet and powerful muscles help them hang on to the hair even when it is combed. Once, more than 16,000 lice were found on one man. They were living not only in his hair but also in his eyebrows and beard.

When an infected person's comb, brush, hat, ribbon, or even earphones are used by someone else, lice spread quickly. Only special shampoos are able to destroy them.

Body lice look very much like head lice but are found only on the body. They feed frequently, each time in a new place. Soon they cause tiny red spots to appear and grow larger. The life cycle of body lice, or "cooties," as they are also called, is the same as that of head lice. Females lay their eggs in the seams of clothing, and the nits cannot survive long after the clothing is removed. While head lice breed in all kinds of places, body lice are found mainly in dirty, crowded ones. They multiply on soiled clothes and on the bodies of those who do not bathe regularly.

Less common are crab lice, which are whitish and smaller than either head or body lice. They live in certain hairy parts of human bodies and have short growths poking out from their sides that make them look like miniature crabs.

All of these lice are fierce hangers-on and are definitely not on anyone's list of favorite insects.

This louse lives on human bodies rather than human heads.

The spicebush swallowtail butterfly can give off a strong smell.

Other Weapons

Not only do all of these (and many other) six- and eight-legged creatures occasionally poke their mouthparts into you, but some have other secret weapons they do not hesitate to use. Some insects are able to spit or spray chemicals, and if you disturb them, you may be in for a smelly surprise.

The spicebush swallowtail butterfly, for example, has two glands behind its head that give off a very strong odor when the butterfly is threatened.

Several kinds of ants are able to spray a foul-smelling substance called formic acid. So too can some cockroaches, beetles, and bugs. These insects could be called the skunks of the insect world.

One relative of the spider, the scorpion, has two poison glands in the tip of its telson, or tail. If disturbed, the scorpion strikes quickly and fiercely. Its sting causes severe pain and sometimes swelling in humans.

The scorpion can deliver a powerful sting with its tail, or telson. There are two poison glands in the telson.

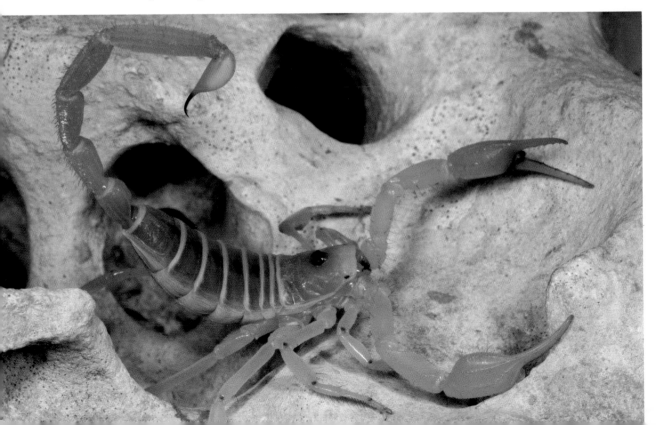

The saddleback caterpillar and the larvae of the io moth have needle-sharp spines on their bodies. If you touch one of these, or rub against it, you will feel a stinging sensation.

This io moth larva has sharp spines on its body. If you brush against them, you'll get stung.

Fire ants can do more than bother you at a picnic. They can give a painful sting.

Many other insects and spiders have clever ways of escaping danger and defending themselves and their young. If a few use their weapons on you, just remember that to the insect or spider, you are a threatening predator.

Of course, it might be hard to appreciate or enjoy insects when one or two choose you for dinner. But at least try to understand. To a hungry little creature, you are a delicious-looking meal.

Scientists who study animals group them together according to their similarities and differences. Animals that have certain features in common are placed in the same **order**. For example, insects in the same order may go through similar stages before they reach adulthood, or they may have the same kind of mouthparts or the same number of wings. There are about 25 orders of insects in all. The orders of some of the insects discussed in this book are described below.

ORDER	MEANING	EXAMPLES	TYPE OF MOUTHPARTS	NUMBER OF WINGS	WHERE USUALLY FOUND
Anoplura	unarmed tail	sucking lice	piercing-sucking	none	on mammals
Diptera	two wings	flies, mosquitoes	larvae: chewing adults: piercing-sucking	2	around plants, animals, food and garbage
Hemiptera	half wings	true bugs, such as bedbugs	piercing-sucking,	4	on plants and flowers
Siphonap-tera	with a tube and wingless	fleas	larvae: chewing adults: piercing-sucking	none	on animals

Glossary

cuticle: the outer skin or covering of some insects

hosts: plants or animals on which parasites live and feed

larva: the young of some insects

maggot: the larva of some insects, such as fleas and flies

molting: shedding an outer skin or cuticle

nits: lice eggs

nymphs: the young of some insects. Nymphs, unlike larvae, usually look like smaller versions of their parents.

order: a group of animals with a number of features in common

parasites: animals that live and feed on other living creatures

proboscis: the mouthparts of certain insects, such as butterflies

pupa: an insect in the pupal stage, the last stage of growth before adulthood

spines: sharp hairs or points on an insect or other animal

spiracles: breathing holes on the bodies of some insects

tumbler: the pupa of mosquitoes

wrigglers: the larvae of mosquitoes

Index

The photographs are reproduced through the courtesy of: pp. 3, 15, 19, 22, 27,
28, 29, 31, 35, 37, front cover (background), back cover, © Robert and Linda
Mitchell; pp. 5, 6, Donald L. Rubbelke; pp. 7, 9, 10, 11, 13, 14, 23, 25, 33, front
cover (inset), Dwight R. Kuhn; pp. 16, 34, © Frank Stibritz; p. 17, Edward S.
Ross; p. 21, © Bill Johnson; p. 36, © John Serrao.